SMARTS

How To
STOP *Worrying About Money*
And
Start Counting It!

Fina Gold and I. M. Greenbacks.

Far-Isles Unlimited, Inc.
1630 30th St., Suite 253
Boulder, CO 80301

i

MONEY SMARTS
HOW TO STOP WORRYING ABOUT MONEY AND START COUNTING IT!

Copyright © 1991
Far-Isles Unlimited, Inc.

Library of Congress Cataloging-in-Publication Number
91-071694

ISBN NUMBER 0-9628717-0-2

ACKNOWLEDGEMENTS:

Our worries were written on scraps of paper, exchanged, and edited by ourselves, looked over by our friends, inspected by professionals, and chuckled at by semi-experts, and brainstormed by anybody we could trick into reading our material.

Ours is only one way of looking at the problem of money and ours might be the only one that deals with the subject of worry. Do whatever it takes to stop worrying about money. Being happy and fulfilled is what the game of life is all about.

A list of suggested reading materials appears at the back of this book. It took us a long time and a lot of reading plus a lot of worrying before we got what it took to change and to produce the results that made us happy again.

OUR SPECIAL THANKS TO:

Dona Haglin, Maureen Larson, Frank Barone, and Diane Olson who proofread our book and gave us inspiration.

Mel Typesetting -:- Denver, Colorado

Marianne Garehime -:- Artist, Denver, Colorado

Johnson Publishing -:- especially to Robin Powers

TABLE OF CONTENTS

ACKNOWLEDGEMENTS III

PREFACE VI

FORWARD 1

1. FACE UP 2
Get real about your money situation. Facing up is the
first step in handling your money problems.

2. IDENTIFY YOUR SITUATION 6
Yee, gads! I have to do this? What is my situation?
Am I poor or am I better off than I thought?

3. FIX A CRISIS STATE 12
Oh, my goodness, it's worst than I thought! Now what?
How do I fix it? Looks as though I'll have to take some
action. Oh, well, let's do it!

4. ORGANIZE YOURSELF 22
Does this mean I have to find the receipts and get them
in order? I have a headache . If only I had done this
from the beginning.

5. SIMPLIFY YOUR KEEPING SYSTEM............ 30
KISS – Keep it simple, sweetie. Get a shoebox, a
notebook, pencils and let's go to work.

6. CAP A WEALTHY STATE **36**
What did I do to deserve this and how do I keep it? Aunt
Harriet said in her will,"Don't to spend all this money
in one place."

7. FIRE UP AN OKAY STATE **42**
Get off your duff and get going.Why accept mediocrity?
You can't win unless you enter the race.

8. WHAT MONEY IS AND IS NOT **48**
Go with the flow. Put out the effort and it will come
back to you in forms beyond your imagination.

9. "BEE" BUSINESSLIKE ABOUT LIFE............ **56**
Don't let it just happen. Plan what you want and be
flexible if things don't work out as you think they
should. Develop another plan.

10. ACT ON YOUR DREAMS...................... **62**
Make it happen. You can do it!

HELPFUL HINTS **68**

READING LIST.................................. **69**
Check it out! There's more — A Reading List, Order Forms, etc.

ORDER FORM................................... **71**

PREFACE

"Let's do something!", my cohort and I concluded after months of crying on each others shoulders about money worries. IT permeated our lives!

We couldn't understand IT! We worked, had an above average paycheck and we were constantly in debt, living off credit cards, and writhing about finances.

We sought quick fix-em solutions, like buying lottery tickets, sending out sweepstakes, or banking on lotto and demanding that LUCK favor us! When it didn't, we'd go for bigger stakes like the stock market and lose our shirts!

We found each other commiserating in misery. We found relief in each other's drama on Friday afternoons, a time when we should have been light-hearted and happy. Instead, we were heavy-hearted and worried!

For months, we stewed, fretted, and wallowed about money worries, each trying to outdo the other. We were sure that nobody, but nobody had it as bad as we did! The woebegones went on until we sized up the truth behind our money worries. By then, our "money block" was the size of the "Berlin Wall".

When we reached the saturation point of dissolution and self-pity, we decided it was time to pull our heads out of hiding and face facts!

We considered ourselves to be intelligent and self-reliant human beings who could find a solution to our money situation.

Our Friday afternoon meetings became serious work sessions! Our money habits came under microscopic scrutiny. With hawk-eyed attention, we started to watch the inflow and the outflow of our checkbooks.

We charted our spending habits and started to change. We met where free munchies were served with drinks. A small start but for us a conscious one! We stopped complaining and started getting together answers to the whys of our money worries!

We addressed questions that hung around like a cloud. Why did we have such a hard time with money? What was the reason behind that anxious feeling whenever someone mentioned money? Why wasn't there ever enough? Why was it so worrisome?

When we met, we came together with reading materials, know how literature, and intellectual questioning. We were determined and we demanded improvement over our finances!

Like modern day Einsteins, we applied the scientific method to our search. Kids, mates, and pleasures were put on hold. "How to Stop Worrying About Money..." took precedence!

We are sure that you will find our concerns true and our solutions worth considering and applying to your life.

To get the most out of reading this book, take time to write "Your Notes, Comments, Thoughts, and Feelings" provided in the designated places.

By personalizing this workbook, it becomes yours. You actually take care of your money worries, thereby casting them off so that you can become lighthearted and worry free.

We did it! We shed our money worries and we think you will too with this common sense, funny book about money.

FORWARD

I. M. Greenbacks, co-author of Money Smarts, has been a close friend of mine for several years, and I was excited when I heard that she and Fina (pronounced Fīna) Gold had their book ready to go to the publisher. I am extremely delighted to have been asked by the authors to write this Forward.

As I read this book, a list of memories came to mind of the many hours we had sharing our thoughts and ideas for increasing our income. I. M. has been one of my strongest supporters and a person who has encouraged me so many times. This book is written in such an enlightening manner that you too can reap the rewards of putting your ideas to work. Money Smarts can be a practical tool for taking the action needed to motivate yourself to start maximizing your income.

I know you will enjoy reading this book and will get as much use from it as I have. Find the skills you have within yourself to start goal setting and work to make those ideas start paying off. I have seen it work for the authors; I know it has worked for me, and now it's time to start making it work for you!

Diane Olson

A Boulder Business Woman

1

FACE UP

The first step to eliminating worry about money is to face up to your own situation, to know what you are dealing with!

Sooooo, gather up your bills, your receipts, your past due notices, warnings, etc. Yes, get it all! This is called facing the truth about your money state. CONFRONT! CONFRONT! CONFRONT!

To face up means no more hiding. It means no more wishful thinking that somehow it will all work out. It won't, unless you take action!

Stop buying lottery tickets, and start gambling on yourself. You got yourself in trouble and you can get yourself out of trouble.

Put the phone down! Your father can't help you. He might have helped the last time but there is a limit to his resources.

Stop worrying, chewing your nails, or taking out your frustrations on the family, or worst yet, in drink or other forms of escape. Also, stop putting yourself down with these silent reprimands!

Maybe it was dumb of you to get yourself in a financial mess. Pat yourself on the back however, for having the courage to face up to it now!

Facing up is not easy! It's hard, very hard! It will make you cringe, but take heart, admit where you are financially, then do something about it. If you have to go through a period where you're angry over your present situation or you want to feel sorry for yourself, then do that and be done with it so that you can move on to other things.

It is hard to change an ingrained habit, and it will feel uncomfortable at first. Sometimes more confusion is generated. Why? Because change and order is new! Your mind does not like change! It's habitual in nature. It would rather have things the way they are even though they are a mess!

A ten year old girl was overheard telling her mother that she liked her room cozy, even though cozy meant everything on the floor, not put away! That was what she was used to!

It's easier to rely on the old habits than to try a new approach. Most of us are so set in our ways that we can't even recognize a better way until we're forced into a predicament where the old ways are not working.

Even then we tend to stay in the same old life style though it may be killing us. We take action only when we have to! We put up, put off, and even suffer rather than try something new. It is so with everyday matters!

When you begin to change, you will have to work hard at turning off the flood of <u>predispositioned</u>, self-programmed thoughts that will attack you, prevent you from changing! Recognize them as such and change anyway!

Start out by admitting, and facing up to the present situation. Humans are not perfect and you're human. The hardest part will be to admit your ways of dealing with money haven't been the way you would like. When you do face up, you will make room for order in your mind.

Financial order begins when you take action over your money problems. It does not mean attacking yourself; it means attacking the problem. Panic and fear will dissolve when you face up and take charge over your money situation.

Start by dealing with your emotions. Face your humiliation, then make a date with yourself, you with you! So it sounds weird! Do it anyway! Make it special as if you are taking out "the one." Find candlelights, etc. Wear your best sweats because you'll sweat a lot when you face your money state!

You'll resist! You won't want to REALLY know the truth about your money. You'll go to the bathroom more than you need to, you'll want to take a shower first, then maybe another one. You'll check out the frig several times, decide to clean your place, talk on the phone, walk your dog or offer to walk you neighbor's dog, if you don't have one!

You'll do anything to avoid facing up! Your mind is used to the OLD you and it will fight to keep the old you even though you want to change. If you've made a habit of ignoring your money state, you will fight to keep that habit. Habits are formed by years of practice. It will take practice to change it!

If your habit of worrying is set and maybe even a natural state for you then worrying will come more naturally for you than resolving your money problem.

Most of us are emotional by nature, not analytical. Being practical is cold and impersonal. Become cold about your money state. Like a chairman of the board take a practical approach, not a dramatic one, when analyzing your money situation.

DATE   IDEAS THAT I CAN USE

_____   _____

                    _____

                    _____

                    _____

SUMMARY: _____
1. Face up to your money situation.
2. Analyze your worry habits.
3. Attack problems, not yourself.
4. Adopt the habit of solving.
5. Study your emotional position.
6. Change your emotional position.
7. Look for solutions.
8. Practice until it's a habit.
9. Avoid drama; think logically.
10. Be mindful of your thoughts.

IDENTIFY YOUR
SITUATION

What is your money position? Bad? Really bad? Desperate? Okay? YOU won the lottery!

At the same time you are trying to figure out your financial status, find a notebook, pencils, an eraser, a ruler, your bills, and your checkbook.

Situate yourself in a quiet place where you can examine your status. If this is an impossible feat to do at home, take yourself to an atmosphere that appeals to you.Wherever you go, take a deep breath and dive in. Make sure you have all of your bills, paid and unpaid. To really see your true financial state, it would be best to have all your expenditures for the past year or several months at your disposal. BORING! True, but someone has to do it. If you found it interesting, you would have done this months ago, and wouldn't be faced with the problems that you are confronting right now. If all your past bills did a disappearing act in the vertical file, now is the time to set up a holding place for the forthcoming ones; a shoe box or a manila folder will do.

Open your notebook and make a ledger. A ledger is an account book, a record of your expenses and a record of your income. The income will be referred to here as "Inflow" and expenses will be known as "Outflow." It will look like this:

Date	Description	Inflow	Outflow
1/1	New Year Bonus	$500.00	
1/1	Champagne		$12.98
1/1	Alka Seltzer		$3.98
1/6	Birthday	$20.00	

By keeping your ledger simple, you are training yourself to do two things: keep track of your "income" and keep track of your "expenses." Learning the money habit is that simple!

Keeping watch over your money should be simple (even though you abhor the shoulds in your life) and it should be fun! It's all a matter of attitude. One page in your notebook might cover a month's entry. List your income under the "inflow" column. Take out your receipts and bills and list them under the "outflow" column.

Don't give in to your mind when it comes up with thoughts of taking a "frig" or "phone" break. Don't give up! Complete at least one month's entry before you give way to any kind of temptation! Throw procrastination out the window and get down to business. Think positive and think how much fun you'll have just accomplishing this project.

After you have done all the posting and can readily view all the "ins" and "outs," add the numbers in each column to show how much money you made and how much money you spent. Subtract your "outs" from the money you brought in, and now you know whether you're in the pink or whether the situation looks rosier than usual. No pun intended.

If your total is a minus number, then you know that something has to be done to get the sides even. Instead of getting mad, putting yourself down, or yelling at the dog, you should learn that you have to do one of two things: increase your inflow or decrease your outflow.

Most of us want immediate gratification; we won't put off tomorrow what we can't afford today, hence our dilemma with money matters.

Of course, if you are getting a monthly allowance from your favorite aunt or won at the dog races this month...well, then you have a different kind of worry. How do I handle a sudden windfall? We'll tell you in the section on wealth.

Why do you think most of us ignore our money situations? Is it possible that there is never enough? We don't want to face reality and possibly if we don't think about it, the situation will go away. If we don't plan for a rainy day, we'll get soaked.

Instead of waiting until trouble slaps you in the face, position yourself to take positive action that will allow you to stay on top of the matter. Be awake to your finances! It should be a process that makes you feel in control, not anxious!

Take a breather, ring out your sweats if you discover that you're in worse shape than you thought. At least you know where you stand and now can take action. Some people, believe it or not, do not even open up their mail from the bank. For example, if they see that the bank has sent them an envelope that has a pink slip showing through the window, they assume their check has been deposited; yellow slips mean that they have overdrawn their account, and a white slip is the account's monthly statement which they never balance anyway, so why take the time to open it. This kind of behavior can lead to trouble. Becoming attentive about your money flow is a step in the right direction.

Maybe you'll become conscious of money for the first time. You'll stop buying on impulse and train yourself to know what you're doing with your money! Maybe you won't be drawn into clever merchandising displays. You'll pass by, not touching anything, and go away feeling very smug about yourself. You've learned that saying no had some very good side effects; you feel good about you.

Taking time to seriously examine your money state will clear up any myths or strange notions that you acquired about money, like "only the rich get richer...", "rich people are unhappy", etc. Being solvent gives one peace of mind and freedom from struggle! Don't let anyone tell you differently!

You'll learn that money is about finding ways to bring it in and finding ways to disperse it in a conscious way. It is keeping track that the inflow is the same, if not more than the outflow.

The first step in handling anything that causes a problem is admitting that there is a problem. Your situation will improve because you know that you have to do something about it. You will improve because you will demand improvement from yourself because you really want it!

DATE   IDEAS THAT I CAN USE

_____   _____

                _____

                _____

                _____

                _____

                _____

                _____

                _____

                _____

                _____

                _____

SUMMARY:

1. Know your money position.
2. Save your receipts and bills.
3. Keep them in a folder, box, etc.
4. Make a ledger, your own account book.
5. Remember, "inflow" is money coming in.
6. Remember, "outflow" is money going out.
7. Keep track of your "ins."
8. Keep track of your "outs."
9. Do NOT ignore your money state!
10. Demand improvement of yourself!

3

FIX A CRISIS STATE

Are you surprised at what you discovered when you posted your expenses and listed your income? Most people are! It shows how blind people are about their money position. It also shows how necessary it is to be mindful and business-like about finances.

Are you worse off than you thought? You feel like you want to get trashed out or at the very least let out a few expletives! Would that help? It might on a temporary basis but eventually reality sets in and the bitter music must be faced. Instead of losing control, think... I have a problem. How do I solve the problem? Don't get emotional... get logical.

Now that ignorance is no longer bliss, the business of solving this problem is on the road to recovery. Celebrate! You are accomplishing your goal!

You've faced up. You know that you have to do something and you are! Give yourself a hug or pat yourself on the back. When you have accomplished your goal, try not to look back and reprimand yourself for not taking positive action sooner. The most important thing is that you're doing it now!

If you declare your financial situation to be a crisis state, meaning traumatic, critical, severe, then you must declare urgency on your part and take immediate action. Your head will be out of hiding, upright for action even though you may be shaking in your boots. If you still need more emotional wailing then do so quickly. Fill a tub full of sudsy water or stand under a pounding shower and bawl or pound your feather pillow, whatever works so that you can get rid of the anxiety to begin afresh.

When your emotions are spent and you're pounds lighter, give yourself a pep talk. Moneywise you drew a lemon. So make lemonade! Our lemon was worrying about money, so we wrote a book to get out of hock! You can do it too! Be creative to find the right avenue for you. Brainstorm until you run out of ideas. Something will show up and give you direction. It always happens that way when your intentions are sincere. If the answers are not coming, relax, and when you go to bed, just ask your inner self to work on the problem. Before you know it, you'll be able to find the right solution.

And if you're still playing mind games with yourself, that you're not smart enough to find an answer, then remember that it's not talent that turns dreams into reality, it's discipline. Talent is not a rare commodity; discipline is.

If you still need a pep talk, take out your notebook, your ledger, and somewhere in the back start a GRATITUDE LOG. List all the things you are grateful for, like snow tires still good for another season or a good babysitter or a helpful mate.

Ask yourself... what are you thankful for? A good marriage? A bad marriage that you fixed? Children? A home? A job that you like? A list of your dreams? There is no better way of getting rid of self-pity than by concentrating on what you do have rather than what you don't have. The list will show you that despite your so-called failures, your character flaws, the mistakes you made, you are getting better. Use the gratitude log to pull yourself out when you're down.

Life is a challenge and getting better at surmounting obstacles is the big test of fortitude. You have to be willing to accept life's encounters. They show up at your front door when you least expect it. If you can do this and still maintain a sense of humor, then you have mastered the ultimate! Joe had severely broken his ankle which meant that he had to have surgery. The day before he was ready to leave the hospital, Joe accidentally fell on his crutches and had to undergo surgery again, but this time the ankle had to be held together by pins and screws. Later the doctor teasingly told Joe that the ankle was so bad that he had to throw away some of the smaller bones. Joe quickly retorted that he shouldn't have done that because his dog could have eaten them. Joe, although in a great deal of pain, was only teasing the doctor back. Joe felt that what happened to him, happened for a reason and there was a lesson for him to learn.

To view life from a humorous point of view is not always easy, but if you can view the happenings as merely challenges for you to overcome, and nothing more, then you can handle these incidences in a very pragmatic way.

Thomas Edison tried nine hundred and ninety-nine times before he invented the electric light bulb. He learned nine hundred and ninety-nine ways what didn't work. During the process of elimination, Mr. Edison came closer to solving the problem. You can produce financial order in your life in a shorter period than it took Mr. Edison to invent the light bulb. Just don't give up!

Now that you have your emotions intact, you're ready to take action to solve your problem. Feel like the chairman of the board; you've got a company problem, meaning you, and you're going to fix it!

To help you along with this calm and serious state that you have reached, remove yourself temporarily from life's daily demands to a quiet place. It can be a den, a corner in a room, or a treehouse. With your notebook in hand, start listing your solutions.

You'll find the natural instinct will be to tighten spending. You'll naturally find yourself listing ways that you can save money. It will seem logical, however, if you concentrate only on economizing your expenses and not producing more income, you'll still be in trouble. Think of ways to generate revenue as the primary area of concern rather than economizing on food, etc. Think instead on what you can do to make more money.

Economizing won't make more money, but producing will. Try getting a second job, having a garage sale or performing a service for someone else. It doesn't have to be forever, just long enough to balance the inflow with the outflow.

You might be thinking that your money situation is so bad that you'll never be out of debt and that it takes money to make money. This might be faster, but you don't have any. Stop THINK-ING about getting rich, start GETTING rich by producing more income.

You can have a continual flow of money only from your own efforts, not from sitting around waiting for handouts! Production is the only way to bring in money. All the rich individuals were able to enmass fortunes because they put their creative juices into action and did something about their situations. You can do the same. All you need to do is to take action.

Remember when you were a teenager, how quickly you were able to come up with money making ideas: a car wash, a bake sale, babysitting, mowing lawns, etc. Take yourself back to that kind of creative thinking when you were willing to do anything to make money. That's the kind of attitude you will need to get yourself out of hock. You can't feel that you're beneath that kind of work.

Feeling embarrassed or ashamed about taking a second job, having a sale of your stuff or performing a service for money won't do. It will take extra work on your part to get you out of the danger zone if you want to become solvent again! Hard work never killed anyone; you may think so, but it hasn't. On the contrary, work revitalizes people. Humans want to be productive, not sedentary. Retired people are starved for something to do.

Be happy that you are able to work!

Stretch your thinking. Explore your interests and your talents. Do you like to write letters? A university student did; he wrote love letters for his buddies and made enough to pay his way through college.

An English teacher who had 130 students a day wanted a quiet job where she could earn extra money for her travel which she loved to do during the summer. She cleaned houses! Are you good at putting together plastic models? Hobby stores will pay you for your patience. Do you like to wax cars? A computer programmer did. It got the kinks out of his neck and gave him a nice side income.

What could you do? A single mother with three children was having a hard time making ends meet. She put the three girls in one bedroom, dormitory style, and rented the other two bedrooms until she got on her feet. The girls had complained at first but later they loved it and the mother had been able to keep a roof over their heads!

If you need money, sell something! Most of us have a surplus of possessions and wouldn't miss the things sold. The money it will bring you will make you feel better and will encourage you to look for other money making ideas.

A good way to come up with money making ideas is to ask around. Two brains are better than one. Another is to brainstorm on paper like you did in junior high English class when you had to generate ideas for a story. Write down whatever comes to mind, then cluster similar thoughts into groups until you have several possible ways for making money.

You won't have to make extra money forever, only long enough to get financially ahead. However, what usually happens is the extra money is nice and makes life more enjoyable. You can take the dream trip you've been thinking about or do the extras you always wanted. The man who liked making models now has his own educational television show teaching others how to do it.

A side benefit that you will discover from generating income from second sources other than your work, is that you will not have idle time on your hands to feel sorry for yourself. Soooo you will profit psychologically as well!

When it's time to retire from your job, you will not be bored because you will know how to make money out of things that you enjoy doing. Colonel Sanders had a seasoning idea for chicken that grew to a full time franchise business, Kentucky Fried Chicken! He was in his seventies when he came up with the idea! It's never too late.

From the large flow of ideas that you'll generate in your notebook, you will keep busy for several life times! It will make you feel like a rich person because you will always have money. Having it allows you to pursue interests, to travel, to seek education, to provide needed services, or to conquer new worlds.

Getting rich is having ideas! The creative process of thinking up ways to make money and making it will make you feel like a master over your life, not a slave to it. The freedom of not having to worry about where your next meal is coming from will allow you to concentrate on developing your personality, becoming a deep sea diver if you wish.

If you still don't have any ideas or if the ideas you came up with aren't producing much money, don't give up or bury your head in the sand! Failures are only outcomes that didn't turn out, YET! Mr. Macy, of Macy's Department store, tried many times before he had what he wanted. You will too, if you persevere and keep going despite the not YET successes.

A father told his son this parable. "Do you remember reading about George Washington?"

"Yes," the son replied.

"Well, he never gave up!" his father stated.

"Do you remember reading about Abraham Lincoln"?

"Yes", said the son.

"Well, he never gave up! Do you remember reading about Arthur Twindledee?" the father continued.

"No", replied the son.

"Well, he gave up."

The point is well made! Are you going to give up because it's hard, will take you longer than you want it to, or you're too tired, discouraged, frustrated, sick of feeling like a loser, etc? No! No! No! Keep going! Incidentally, Abraham Lincoln tried many times before he won his place in the political arena!

After putting ALL of your energies on finding ways to produce more income, only then do you ECONOMIZE. If you start by economizing you'll become frustrated and give up because there's not enough money to go around. You have to find a way to make more money first to balance your ins with your outs; then you can look at ways to economize and find out where you are wasting money.

DATE   IDEAS THAT I CAN USE

_____   _____

               _____

               _____

               _____

               _____

               _____

               _____

FIX A CRISIS STATE

SUMMARY:

1. Accept your crisis state.

2. Take time to unleash your emotions.

3. When you're done, fix your crisis state.

4. Declare a state of urgency and work to resolve it.

5. Produce ways to increase income first.

6. Economize after you have made extra money.

7. Make lemonade if handed a lemon.

8. Like discipline. It's mastery over self.

9. Make and use your gratitude diary.

10. Brainstorm ways to make money.

ORGANIZE
YOURSELF

To find out where to economize and where you are wasting money takes some form of plotting, organization. What does being organized mean?

Some of you may be grinding your teeth at the sound of the word! Being a person who doesn't like to live by the clock or be scheduled, you probably yawn and say, BORING!

A reformed alcoholic who didn't like regulating his life asked his friend, "How can I go through the Christmas season without a drink?" he whined. "It wouldn't be any fun!"

"That's true," his friend replied. "It was a lot of fun seeing you get drunk, puking on the carpet, and then yelling at everyone. It's too bad you don't remember how much fun WE all had."

To organize means to provide yourself with structure. That's a word you are absolutely certain you don't want to hear. It connotes images of your mom getting after you to clean your room or your dad yelling at you because you didn't know what you wanted out of life even though you were an adolescent!

What's this organized stuff? YOU know what it means! What? Ugh...ugh, well. You never had to put it in words before. It's action, not procrastination. It's getting your life affairs in order so that you can go on and accomplish all the things you want.

Organizing your money life is necessary despite the charge the word *organize* might bring up for you. To diffuse any emotional attachment you might have towards a word, look up the true meaning in a dictionary instead of going by associated meanings. Think about the word *mother-in-law*. What comes to mind? Need we say more?

Knowing the literal meanings also extends your vocabulary and increases your I.Q.! Malcom X spent most of his prison term copying the entire dictionary from A to Z! The nearly illiterate man became intellectually refined as a result of this process.

Let's take the word *organize*. According to the dictionary it means, "provide yourself with an organic structure." What does *organic* mean and who really cares? Unfortunately, it's a necessary evil if we want to eliminate the confusion in our lives and if we want more tranquility in our environment. So, let's bite the bullet and carry on.

Organic means "to systematically arrange or to implement," whereas *structure* means "building, to heap together or arrange." Now the word *organize* becomes a little clearer.

By clarifying meanings of words, you actually personalize your understanding of them. They become custom fitted to your level of knowing. Clearing up meanings of words also can be enhancing. When you get what a word really means to you, you feel more in tune, more intellectually enlightened, and more in control.

But, when you are confused by a meaning, you actually go into nervous hysteria because you're trying to make sense of it. Recall a time when you were in school and you didn't have a grasp of what the teacher or the text was saying. How did you feel? If you were like the rest of us, you shut off mentally! You became blank.

You probably did something similar when your mother asked you to clean your room. To you, it probably meant spring house cleaning whereas all she probably wanted you to do was to pick the stuff off the floor.

We learned intellectual and emotional meanings of words from our parents, teachers, and our society. We froze these meanings in our minds where they are stuck for life unless we re-evaluate them. A linguistic professor was so concerned with this kind of mental hardening that he took a two year leave of absence to study his own use of words!

He learned that he was using words to express what he really meant, and that he was not really certain what word to use to express what he really felt. And in some cases he didn't know what he really felt! His research pointed to the psychological power of words and the effect they have on people. If you doubt it, recall a time when you were really angry with your spouse or your children. You hurt them with words as if you hit them physically!

Labeling people hurts too. It distances them from you. The Civil Rights movement in the 60's unleashed cruel words. Unleash the labels you have on words by looking them up and using them exactly! If you do, then maybe the word *organize* may not mean what you think it means.

A woman of means thought *organize* meant waking up at noon, lunching late, and spending the day with her friends! To us, the working class, *organize* means: setting the alarm for an early wake; eating breakfast on the run; working until quitting time; and resting a bit to do it all over again!

Think what "get organized" means to you. The dictionary says "get" means "to obtain, to become the owner of, acquire, gain, to arrive at, to catch, commit to memory." Which fits your point of view? Which one will make you get organized? Which one will forever oust the emotional hold it has on you?

If *get organized* means "provide a structure" and *structure* means "to arrange" and *get* means "to obtain" then maybe the phrase "get organized" will be easier for you to swallow!

The point here is to disassociate and discharge psychological meanings you have brought to words so that you can set aside your defenses when words come up, clear up the association, and do the things that need to get done.

To one person get organized might mean "to institute a plan," to another simply "get order"! If you are a person who doesn't have order in your life, this word will bring a charge on you and make you feel uncomfortable! *Order* has twenty three meanings of which some are: "to arrange, to organize, to manage, to direct." The surest way to rid yourself of an emotionally packed word is to know its wide range of meanings!

Antonyms or opposite meanings can crystallize meanings too. *Disorder* is the opposite of *order*. Its meanings are: "bewilderment, defeat, and disarrangement." Looking up words that make you fidget is psychologically therapeutic!

From an antonym point of view, *get organized* means "eliminating confusion," which may be your first step toward achieving order! What order signifies to one person may not be to another. A hostess at a Thanksgiving dinner fixed a lot of mashed potatoes. Her husband, an engineer, asked how she had calculated the number of potatoes she needed for the dinner. "Did you take the square root of their stomachs, divide by two...?" he asked her. "No, dear, I didn't do that. I didn't even think of doing that! I just peeled the potatoes until I finished the sack."

The importance a person attaches to something is contingent upon the thing being considered. You won't procrastinate, you will make quick decisions, and you will get things done if order is important to you! Most of us would like to reach that state. It is our reason for writing this book.

To be ordered is a thing we work towards at varying degrees. Eliminating confusion in our lives is a peace we want. It takes patience to put order where disorder reigns. It doesn't come about all at once. A switchboard operator can only handle one light at a time. A good one does it calmly, dealing with one call at a time; eventually she answers all the calls.

Right now, in this book, you are giving money worries your full attention and it should be so! To get rid of the confusion that you will have about money, you must be able to look at all your personal slants towards money.

One of these bends may be towards muddled thinking about keeping records, being organized, or not caring about money. Maybe you think that if you act like money doesn't mean anything, you can convince yourself that you always have more than you need. Or maybe you think like the busy businessman who couldn't keep his desk clean. He bought a sign which read: "The sign of a sick mind is a clean desk." He can't fool anyone; he was trying to justify his disorder! Maybe you judge people by how much money they have. And since you don't have much, it makes you feel worthless. A high price to pay for such thinking!

Maybe you believe that big money is only for the rich. Maybe you buy everything in sight to compensate for not having what you wanted as a child. Maybe you think you should have a M.B.A. to manage your checkbook. Maybe, maybe...there are countless of explanations one can find to justify a particular position one holds about money!

Maybe you simply don't want to admit your own shortcomings so that you can go around and around getting further behind and more worried. You may have to start by practicing order in your physical world first to arrive at having order in your money world. If you have to clear off your desk or pick up the stuff off the floor or make peace with your spouse to think clearly, then do it!

If you have to admit to yourself that you don't know math and never did even when you were in school, then admit it and sign up for another math class!

Accept your situation, then do whatever is necessary to make your money life worry free, and even wonderful! Don't spend any negative energy worrying or whining. Spend that time being positive, looking for solutions instead. Do something! If you're going bald, have a pot belly, a Reuben figure instead of a Twig, more bills than income; accept your condition then do something!

A wife nagged her husband for leaving his underwear on the floor every morning. He never did anything about it so having had enough, she nailed them to the floor! You can imagine his surprise when he finally couldn't stand to see them there and went to pick them up!

Do the same, change what you don't like! Design your life like an artist arranges the colors on his canvas, precisely. Greeks design their lives every seven years. They can't blame anyone for the way it turned out. You can't either if your money life is not the way you wanted. You can change it!

And it doesn't matter how much or how little you have. A man who made $200,000 a year sought the help of a Consumer Credit Service. He was near bankruptcy! He had no idea where money went. It's not how much you have; it's how you manage what you have.

When your life is organized, you feel free from worry. You are able to set up pursuits that have meaning to you. It can be a search for a relationship, time to be with your family, helping mankind, expressing yourself through your interests, or seeking greater meanings. Your time on earth is limited; don't waste it on worrying.

Getting your disorder into order can be fun because the end result will make sense to you, systematized like organizing the garage. It feels great afterwards! After you achieved order, vow never to procrastinate again!

DATE   IDEAS THAT I CAN USE

_____   _____

                 _____

                 _____

                 _____

                 _____

                 _____

                 _____

                 _____

                 _____

SUMMARY:

1. Find a workable structure.

2. Learn dictionary meanings of words.

3. Personalize word meanings.

4. Diffuse emotional meanings of words.

5. Know what "get organized" is for you.

6. Know your personal thoughts on money.

7. Find your shortcomings.

8. Fix your shortcomings.

9. Fix one thing at a time.

SIMPLIFY
YOUR KEEPING
SYSTEM

Your organizational plan can be simple or elaborate depending on your personal sense of style. For some, a record keeping system could be a shoebox, for others a computer! The method by which you record your income, expenses, budget, etc., doesn't matter; what does is that you do it!

One of the first things you will want to know is your net worth. To calculate it is easy. Simply list what you OWN and what you OWE. Give each item a dollar value, then add up both sides and subtract the difference which is your net worth.

NET WORTH	
What you OWN	**What you OWE**
Car.................................1500.00	Borrowed money from friend 500.00
Furniture 3000.00	Credit Cards 1200.00
Clothes 1000.00	Credit Union......................... 500.00
Savings.............................. 300.00	
	...............*And so on* ....
...............*And so on*...........................	

The net worth is a financial representation of your money worth. If it's not what you want, then you got your work cut out for you. Before you get too down on yourself, remember that you have more than you did in high school!

Knowing where you are money-wise will help you understand where you want to be money-wise and what plan you must initiate to get there.

At the back of the book are forms to order record keeping charts. You can also devise your own system or buy some from an office supply store. Whatever form it takes, use it!

A PERSONAL BALANCE SHEET shows your net worth. A CASH FLOW SHEET shows your cash inflow and outflow. A FINANCIAL RECORDS FILE shows your total financial history. Don't get bogged down in the terminology. You don't have to be a professional bookkeeper or an accountant to understand your money situation. Just think of it as money coming in and money going out. A high school graduate was getting ready to get his own apartment and live on his own. His parents were nervous about Tad being able to make it living on his own. He had a job and had money coming in. Tad reassured his parents by saying, "What's the big deal! I'll have money coming in. All I have to do is pay attention to how much is going out!"

It's really that simple! As we get older we get lost in the maze of our accumulation and desires and often end up with more than we really need. Taking a look at what we really want to be in life and what we want to do is part of simplifying. Most of us buy things because it's a good deal, "It was on sale!" Did we really need it? It still cost something. You have to find a place for it in your home. Americans are known to have more "stuff" than they really need.

Taking a general outlook at yourself is part of simplifying your system, your mode of living. A friend of ours has a big house and it's so crowded with things she bought on sale that there is literally no room to move. There are paths from one room to another. It looks like a used furniture store rather than a home. She's always in debt and she's always buying more "stuff"! WHY?

Those are the kind of questions you have to ask yourself. Do you really need more "stuff" or do you really need to get rid of it?

List what you want to be. What kind of person would you like to be? What do you have to do to become that person? What is it that you really want to have? A lot of things or just a few choice things. List what it will cost money-wise to become that person and the time it will take to become the person you would like to become.

THINGS I WANT TO BE   COST$

_____

_____

_____

_____

_____

THINGS I WANT TO DO   COST $

_____

_____

_____

_____

_____

THINGS I WANT TO HAVE   COST$

_____

_____

_____

_____

_____

You've listed your dreams and how much they will cost to attain. Now list them again and when you would like to achieve them. The reason we have you listing them again is to reinforce in your mind that you really do want them. Give each item a priority factor; which do you want first?

THINGS I WANT TO BE   WHEN

_____

_____

_____

_____

_____

THINGS I WANT TO DO   WHEN

_____

_____

_____

_____

_____

THINGS I WANT TO HAVE   WHEN

_____

_____

_____

_____

_____

Congratulations! You've faced up to your critical situation; you
know your net worth; you found a way to get organized; you're
keeping track of your inflow and outflow; you have a complete history of your financial records: real estate, will, bank accounts, etc.;
and you listed what you want to achieve with the rest of your life,
what you want to be, do, and have statements to measure it!

You'll achieve your financial status because it's no longer a mystery. You know exactly where you stand financially. It's really that simple!

DATE   IDEAS THAT I CAN USE

_____   _____

                          _____

                          _____

                          _____

                          _____

                          _____

                          _____

                          _____

                          _____

                          _____

                          _____

SUMMARY:

1. Calculate your NET WORTH.

2. List what you OWN and OWE.

3. Keep a cash flow sheet for "ins" and "outs."

4. Compile a complete financial records file.

5. List your life goals.

6. Congratulate yourself for doing the above.

7. Keep your system simple.

8. Vow that you will keep up the momentum.

9. Record on a regular basis.

10. Establish good financial habits.

CAP A
WEALTHY STATE

Bill inherited $80,000 from his parents' estate. He quit his job and lived off the money for two years. Although he lived royally, he was shocked at how quickly he went through that inheritance.

Though $80,000 is not wealthy these days, it is still a lot of money. What would you do if you had a windfall, say a lotto win? Would you be any different?

You might be thinking that this is a stupid chapter because you will never have this kind of problem! Let's pretend that you do.

It is fun to pretend. Being a practical sort of person, you would definitely not quit your job, buy a lot of things, give away money to feel like a rich man, nor do anything irrational!

Good. Even a million dollar win will run dry! Sooo not changing your lifestyle for a while is exactly what you should do!

Pay off every bill is the only thing you should do and continue buying only what you need as you did before this windfall. Most people would be inclined to do the opposite but you are the sensible sort and will economize instead.

In a crisis state, the no money state, one's inclination would be to economize; however you learned that you must produce instead because you can't make money without money. Your billfold was bulging. The tax refund you received went fast! Remove that temptation to let it all slip away by capping it immediately. Put a cap over it by putting it in a bank until you can make a rational decision.

You can see a glass of water. How do you perceive that glass? Is it half empty or half full? Your ability to take charge of your life will get you out of the victimization mode and your attitude will determine how effectively you mobilize and redirect your energies toward your activities.

Who are you like? When you have money, your mind knows it and it will not let you have it! It will think up all sorts of things you must buy because it is on sale, it will argue with you. In your new status, it will convince you to buy a new house, a better car, a.... Do not listen to the clever nag, discipline yourself or life will, when it's all gone!

To discipline means to train yourself to do what you deem appropriate. It means to drill yourself to do something that you don't want to do. It means to exercise mentally to adhere to what you want to achieve. It means to regulate your behavior.

If you don't regulate your big cash flow and control your temptations to play, you will lose it for sure! Your mind will not let you keep it because it's not used to you having money. It is a mental system that operates on habit. Your past routine was one of struggle in the matters of money; it will fight to keep you there.

To economize means to take care of your money. The word *economics* is an old word stemming from the idea of managing a household. That's what you will need to do to manage your million with economics in mind.

After you have paid off ALL your bills and capped your windfall in a safe place, go to a quiet place to deliberate why you were given a wealthy state. What did you do to earn it?

In your notebook write down why you think it happened to you. We are big advocates of writing things down because writing is teaching your mind. And if you know the workings of your mind, you will be better able to control the thoughts that pass through it, particularly the negative, debilitating ones, the ones that hurt and weaken your ability to function successfully.

It is through your mind that you command how you want your body to represent itself: confident, timid, fearful, rich or poor. If you order your mind to think thin, it will because it is only a network of facts, like a data bank from which to draw on and act out.

You will feel thin and dispatch a thin image even though you are thirty pounds overweight! Eventually you will eat as a thin person and exercise to convert fat into muscle.

Your mind is nothing more than a collection of experiences you've had and the perceptions you've formed based on these experiences. You can change these new perceptions, new thoughts.

You are a composite of mind, body, and spirit. Your mind is the computer bank that stores everything that happens to you, good and bad. You decide which one to put more emphasis on, no one else! Your body is the visual mechanism by which you act the you, the "spirit" inside you. The personality that we see is the act you play out to show your character and the spirit that resides in you.

It is no different than a house you select to live in; it says something about you as a person. So does the act you put out there for people to see! When you change so does the act and you do change! By changing you can leave a negative situation because you feel you deserve better.

You are changing right now. You are wealthy! Your job at this moment is to reflect on why you have become so: maybe taking time out for an odd aunt paid off, maybe you won the sweepstakes because you didn't give up, or maybe you've admitted to the truth of your money situation!

Maybe it's because you persisted through the hard times, the times when you doubted your abilities and pushed yourself forward despite the put downs your mind was generating to keep you from succeeding.

Maybe you stuck with a marriage you believed in despite your mate's ugly stage. Maybe you're a kind person who cares about the environment. Possibly you've been a rogue who decided to turn over a new leaf.

When you exhausted your findings, record them in your notebook so that you can repeat the same success patterns. With your record of why you think you received good fortune, your bills paid off, and a nest egg capped in the bank, you can feel real good about yourself! Wowee!

When you leave your quiet place, you should expect to be hounded by brokers to invest in their funds. Don't do anything but economize; remember that is the answer to take in the wealthy state. ECONOMIZE!

Your windfall is a seed from the sky which you received for being you! It is your responsibility to sow it wisely so it will produce for you a life time income which you dreamed about so long!

Like a careful gardener, lay out a plan that will produce the best possible crop. If you want to invest in a business, seed your money in service oriented businesses ONLY. Offer a service that others are willing to pay for.

To find out what kind of service that might be, take a tally of your interests and talents. What would you truly like to offer others for which they would be willing to pay? If you you like growing plants, would owning a greenhouse be a service you would like to provide the community? Maybe you could extend your ideas to include laying out gardens in the summer for working couples who do not have time to do so, but would enjoy maintaining an existing garden. Possibly you could start a pooper scooper service and at the same time collect fertilizer for your own organic garden. Be creative!

Do you love, really love exquisite cars? You could start out with a few that needed work, hire teenagers from an auto mechanics school to work on them after school and you'd be providing work for your community as well as producing a beautiful product that others would be willing to pay for.

Investing in only service oriented ventures does several things: it supplies a need; provides employment; and gives you an opportunity to build your capital.

Businesses do fail for several reasons; however if you do what truly interests you and you find a need to fulfill for which people are willing to pay, your chance for success is high.

DATE   IDEAS THAT I CAN USE

_____   _____

               _____

               _____

               _____

               _____

               _____

SUMMARY:

1. Cap your wealthy state.

2. Pay off your bills.

3. Buy only what you need.

4. Don't buy anything extra now.

5. Economize. Become watchful.

6. Discipline yourself not to spend.

7. Don't give into the wanting to spend.

8. Train yourself mentally.

9. Write down reasons for the windfall.

10. Use wealth to set up a service oriented business to make more money.

Fire Up
an
Okay State

If you're one of the so called normal people who are not in a desperate or wealthy state, money-wise that is, but are tired of your stand still position, then you're in the okay position, which is not really okay. Is it?

You trudge to work day in and day out never getting anywhere. You pay your bills every month and have some left over for a movie or to eat out. At this point you might want to consider hiring a good tax accountant, financial planner, or lawyer to help you maximize what you have.

No one wants to just stand still in life! At least in the crisis state your adrenalin goes up because you have to take immediate action. In the wealthy state your elation runs high because you have a lifetime chance to make your life as you desire! You act alive in both states but not so in the okay ho hum state!

It is a weary state; you wear yourself out worrying about all the "what ifs." What if inflation comes? What if an unexpected situation arises? What if you lose your job?

You have to get off dead center! Produce something, something that will give you an additional income as a buffer so that you won't have to worry about all the what if disasters!

And looking for a way to do that will get you out of the middle class worry syndrome. You'll be well on your way to an adventure of discovering interests that you never thought you had, as well as making money from them.

Producing income from a hobby or an interest that you never thought you had, as well as making money from them can be an exciting adventure.

Producing income from a hobby or an interest will be more fun than being a watchdog over a small amount that most of us have left over after we pay all the bills.

It may take some pushing on your part to get out of the doldrums, the just okay state. In this state you are prone to lazy habits: watching television; lying around instead of walking; eating when you don't need to; etc.

No one really likes being stuck in a rut. It's our nature to be energetic and busy. Remember how wonderful it feels when you are that way? We'll unconsciously stir up something, even trouble, to feel alive!

Jack, who left his marriage, did so because he stopped making it exciting. In his new partner, the newness wore off after a couple of years and he was stuck with the same bored feelings.

Margaret left her mundane existence by running away with a man from Los Angeles. She thought it would put zing into her life. When the zing went away, so did Margaret!

A teenager who seeks the wrong group of peers does it for the same reasons: BOREDOM!

That's what the okay state is and it's not okay! Why do you think society worships heroes, athletes, and movie stars? For their status quo? No, they refuse to be middle class, safe, routine.

You can step out of the ho hum life by making things happen for you all the time! Waiting for the knight in shining armor or the pot of gold is just that, waiting! It's the doing that produces results!

Do something, even if it's wrong, but be intelligent about any decision that you make. Do your homework and collect your data in order to insure a reasonable amount of success. By taking action, more action will result, and the right solution or activity will surface. It will give meaning, purpose to your to your life and a chance to have success.

Your argument of where does one find the time or energy won't work! When you know what excites you, you'll be amazed how quickly time and energy will show up!

Most of the working population lives in the okay state. Only 5% of the people are realizing their dreams by doing the extra. The rest live in a day in, day out type of rut.

It will not be easy to drag yourself from the routine you have established as it takes at least two weeks of continually doing something different to make this new pattern a habit.

Persevere! While you're disciplining yourself, build a dream fund by selling things you don't need anymore. The money you gain will stir up dreams you'd like to do.

Instead of feeling sorry for himself, Rob, who became disabled from his brick laying job, experimented with a cookie recipe that he loved. He gave them out to potential customers and now has a thriving business making three times the amount that he did bricklaying! He's dreaming about apple pies now and drawing cartoons in his spare time.

What do you like to do? Amy, a successful banker, wanted to live in a small town and work outdoors. She also loved animals. She started a pick-up service for dogs which now equals her banking job! For just the cost of an ad in the newspaper, Amy gets to be outdoors, plays with animals and is involved in a lucrative business.

Harry was burned out on teaching after twenty years, left his classroom and used his retirement money to become a realtor.

Leav, a Swedish woman who was a graphic designer, dreamed of being a writer in a cabin in the woods. She couldn't afford to quit her job to do it but she could afford a cabin, Ernest Hemingway style. She bought one and spends all her extra time there writing. When she makes enough sales, she'll move there permanently.

Harry and Sue, owners of a small manufacturing company, love going to the flea markets. They have collected enough fine junk to open a second hand store which they did! They are making money and having a lot of fun at it as well as providing a service for the community. Out of this money, they bought an old, teak boat that they are busy refurbishing. They'll probably go into the boat business next!

These people are never without money or something to do! NEVER! They are not bored or just doing okay. They don't worry or wallow in self-pity because they are too busy producing!

Do the same, concentrate on producing instead of worrying over your small funds!

DATE   IDEAS THAT I CAN USE

_____   _____

                   _____

                   _____

                   _____

                   _____

                   _____

                   _____

                   _____

SUMMARY:

1. Doing just okay is not okay.

2. Being just okay is boring.

3. Being okay is standing still.

4. Become active instead of okay.

5. Find something that interests you.

6. Produce money from this interest.

7. Look for a service that people want.

8. Let this service produce this income.

9. Stop being just okay. PRODUCE.

WHAT MONEY IS
AND
IS NOT

Money is something everyone wants and few have it. Do you really know what money is?

It is a convenience developed by modern societies to replace the bartering system. It's easier to carry around bills and coins than to carry a dozen eggs to exchange for a loaf of bread!

This exchange process is still used in less developed cultures. Children barter naturally: a toy for a toy; candy bar for a pop; a pop for chips, etc. Using coins and paper bills is a convenient method of exchanging for goods, services, or benefits wanted.

Money is a reciprocating process, an act of substituting one thing for another. It is not something mysterious! It is bills and coins, currency stamped out by governments to be used by its citizens as a medium of exchange for goods and services they desire.

It is simply a symbol for things we want to have. It is not a magical commodity bestowed on the privileged few. The pot of gold these people have came out of their efforts not from some mystical source that we tend to assume.

Waiting for a pot of gold or a lotto win has become a national pastime. We think the windfall comes from sources outside ourselves. It doesn't!

Money is a factor of production. When you give your time or produce a service for someone, you receive payment for doing it. A contractor builds a home for someone; a secretary types a letter for a company; a realtor finds a home for a client.

Riches result through hard work, perseverance, and determination. Huge empires did not come about by talking about them. You do not get something for nothing. Waiting for wins is that kind of attitude!

It is a faster way but unlikely for most of us! You'd probably get your pot of gold faster if you applied yourself to producing something that will result in money for you!

The mystical thinking about money results from not seeing that money results directly from the product produced. When we were an agricultural society, we could see the tie between harvests gathered and the money it produced in the market.

In our grandparents' days, those who lived on farms saw clearly what provided food on the table, work! They raised chickens and meat, grew vegetable gardens, and exchanged with their neighbors for goods they produced.

We, on the other hand, have come to think of work as some kind of drudgery, a burden from which we want to retire as soon as possible! Yet, those who do, wish they had something more meaningful to do.

When Tim's father retired, he was so bored that he rearranged his wife's kitchen to which she promptly retorted, "Find something to do!" He did! He made a beehive and now has a thriving honey business!

Don't reach out for magic handouts, luck, sugar daddies, or lottery wins! Do something that will result in money. Even the tiniest of human beings want to be productive!

Idle is not what humans want to be. The idle rich who jet aimlessly from one party to another are no different from those who are incarcerated. They are hardened by lack of purpose in their lives. They drink, abuse drugs, and have sex for lack of something to do. The fathers of these rich people who built these empires did so through hard work and they didn't have time to be idle; they were too busy.

Idleness means being in a state of inactivity, dawdling, time-killing. That's not what you want! Remember your first paycheck babysitting or mowing a lawn? How did it feel? Susan's thirteen year old daughter told her mother that she liked fixing the family dinner because it made her feel useful, valuable.

It is human nature to exchange something for something. Have you ever received and never paid back, maybe when your parents paid your debts and there was never any money left at the end of the month to repay them. Did you feel comfortable or guilty? They possibly contributed to these uncomfortable feelings by not insisting on the money due them.

If work represents money received, then the amount of work you produce is relative to the amount you receive. We hate to admit that money is the person, but to some degree, it's true.

The amount of money we receive is dependent on our abilities and our needs. We all need shelter, food, and clothing. Whether it's a tent or a mansion, a buffet or a banquet, a plain wrap or a mink depends on one's preferences and one's abilities.

Also, much of what we want depends on the position we want to hold among the populace. Egos vary!

If the big time is your thing, go for it! You can choose the game you want to play but be realistic about what it takes: education, family status, talent, brains, money. Develop what it takes to have it. You probably can do it because you thought of it!

If you think that lots of money will make everything all right, then go for it, but before you do, try to figure out what it is about money that will make you feel that way. Just sitting in your living room with your riches, won't do it, will it? Is it that it will buy you status? Freedom to do what you really want? Is it to get you out of debt? Out of a job you really hate?

It is important that you know what you need so you don't lose sight of your goals.

You may not have to wait for money in order to do what you desire. Life really is just a series of things to do, obstacles to overcome, and goals to set. If you doubt it, think of the older folks in your family, what have they achieved, what have they had to overcome, and what do they still have to achieve?

Don't waste time dawdling and worrying, start producing the results you want in your life! Don't merely endure a situation, take action.

If you really don't know what you want to do in life, then go back to the time when you really enjoyed something! Was it helping your dad build a bird house? Or was it helping your mom in the garden? Really dig for an answer because whatever it was, it made you feel alive! That's how you should feel most of the time now regardless of your environment! If you don't, change it! When you are doing what you like you are happy and so are the people around you.

Opportunities will show up sooner when you are contented, confident. People will draw to you like bees to honey. Everyone wants to be around confident and happy people because they want some of the happiness for themselves! You'll have more energy to produce more, love more, be more!

You will become a hero! People will love you because you are doing what you love! Like the stars who get paid for just showing up, so will you. You'll be running your life like a race, a race that's going somewhere! Your love will give you all the money you need.

When we yearn for money instead of work, we are yearning for someone to take care of us. A spouse? An institution? Whatever? They will but they will also make the decisions for us! Some of us think that when we are taken care of that it is love. It is not! It means that you are afraid to take care of yourself for fear that you won't do as good a job as your mom or dad did!

Taking care of yourself is risky. It means being accountable for your mistakes and failures, or achieving greatness! If you do nothing and let others do it for you, then you can blame them if it doesn't turn out right.

The risk of failing hangs over most of us like a storm cloud! We are afraid to fail! Stars and athletes who try again and again before they succeed are good models for getting rid of this fear we all have.

The stars that we all admire learned early that the best antidote for fear is action, after that more action!

Action is a state of doing something. It is accomplishing or achieving which produces results in your life. Think back to a time when you did just that and again to a time when you did not. It felt like putting life off. That's exactly what you are doing when you're not producing results in your life.

Your life is either a work of art or a work of chaos. When the people in a culture work, the individuals are rich and happy because there is a flow of exchange of doing something for something.

This network of producing is a network of exchange, of communicating through work. It is energy at its best like a mountain stream flowing down hill to make a lake. It is a circular exchange of pure energy and aliveness.

Money flows out of production. It's cycles of actions produced by individuals in group form to result in an end product for which others are willing to pay. This cycling process makes our economy strong and healthy and the individuals who reside in it, powerful.

SUMMARY:

1. Know what money really is.

2. Don't consider it to be mysterious.

3. Don't think it's only for the rich.

4. Exchange money for goods and services.

5. Work for the pot of gold.

6. Work to produce food on the table.

7. Work to buy services you desire.

8. Work to be productive.

9. Work to get rid of idle time.

10. Work to produce money; find a balance in life.

DATE   IDEAS THAT I CAN USE

_____

_____

_____

_____

_____

_____

_____

_____

_____

_____

_____

_____

_____

_____

_____

_____

_____

_____

_____

_____

_____

"BEE"
BUSINESSLIKE
ABOUT LIFE

Bees know what they're up to in their lives. Do you know what you're up to? Years pass by leaving most of us to wonder what happened. What have you produced thus far and where do you want to go?

Most companies would be out of business if they didn't have a business plan and if they didn't establish their goals. Just letting things happen is foolish. "BEEing" businesslike about your life means setting a course for yourself, a plan.

You can't reap any results until you have set a straight sail for yourself. Know the future you are aiming for. Know what your life business is! Choose something even if it ends up being the wrong thing.

Jan wanted to quit teaching to try her hand at being a stock broker. It took her three years to make the break! When she finally did, she wondered why it had taken her so long as she had truly found her direction in life!

Rick was spinning his wheels. He tried fixing cars from his garage but his interest waned and he decided he wanted to become a realtor. When he couldn't make a quick sale, he gave up and took a paying job! That didn't occupy him long, so he took three months from his life to travel out of his van to find himself. He did, in Florida where he fixes boats. He hopes to have a boat business. He found his direction.

A course of action clarifies your place of being. Even when the going gets rough, you won't give up because you know where you are going. The rough waters you will encounter will be traversed; you won't let them debilitate you. You'll keep on sailing.

Only 5% of the population know where they are going. The rest of us have not looked at our short term goals, let alone put together a long term plan of what we will be accomplish in the future. Thinking about the future means thinking about choices, taking risks, having a plan and working the plan.

Most of us have formed habits of letting things happen. We react rather than act. We're afraid of making the wrong decision so usually we make no decision. It's difficult to realize that by making no decision, we have made a decision and that decision was to have everything remain status quo.

Not taking responsibility for the way our lives are turning out is copping out! Zack, who is in his forties, is still blaming his father for the way his life turned out. Zack's father inherited a family business that went bankrupt. Zack planned on living a rich son's life when suddenly all his dreams tumbled with the collapse of the family business. He resented having to go to work to support himself.

It's better to try many decisions than to try none. You're bound to come up with a solution that suits you. You won't if you brood and do nothing.

When you don't have the outcome you want, regroup and try another course of action and another until you get the results you want.

All successful people failed in some cases but failure was not in their vocabulary; it was that some choices did not work out and that was only one less way to try to reach their goal.

You have to recondition yourself not to think of failure but believe the outcome you want is possible. Don't put yourself down; it only drains your energy and prevents you from functioning!

The literal meaning of failure is "an unsuccessful attempt," and nothing else. It doesn't mean the person is a failure but that the attempt was unsuccessful. Try another one if the idea didn't work out.

When the outcome is not what you want, analyze it like a business would, then set a new course of action. Do not give up until you have reached your destination.

If being rich is your goal, know how you're going to get there. Set up a step by step plan how you will accomplish this, and then don't let anyone deter you from that goal by promising quick riches. There will always be an opportunity for good deals, so work your plan and make your dreams come true.

The results you want will happen if you persist! An Australian author who wanted to be a writer since she was seventeen years old stuck to her plan despite her outcomes. It took her thirty three years to become the writer she wanted! Today she is a highly regarded novelist.

Be specific about what you want. A man of the Polish gentry lost his position, his wealth, and his country during the Second World War. He knew he could not regain his status because he had no money, no skills, plus had to cope with a language barrier when he and his family moved to the United States. He did the next best thing, made sure his children received a good education. It gave him pleasure seeing his children become educated, acquiring the abilities and the skills to succeed.

"BEEing" businesslike is advancing with a purpose. Your intentions have to be clear and explicit. Before a business person's dreams are realized, he/she drafts a plan, a program of what he/she intends. He/she executes each function on a time line so that he/she knows what needs to be done and when he/she needs to have that accomplished. It can't be a hit and miss situation or it won't work.

When you are advancing with a purpose, your life is composed and easy to manage. Design your life as carefully as an artist or a businessman. Arrange it with artistic effort. Think it out beforehand. Don't just let it accidentally happen, but be flexible to change if things aren't going as you had planned.

Map out your life in all areas including your relationships, not just your occupation. Put order in your life in all of your places of being: yourself, your job, your possessions, your spirit, and your environment. You get back what you put into things, so find a balance in life so that no one area suffers.

Each of us lives in our own little world and creates our own perceptions of how life should be within that world. It is our personal viewpoint. Whenever another person describes his or her world, it becomes threatening because it might be different from our perception of the way things should be organized. Tolerance is the key and the knowledge that we can only affect things in our environment and have some semblance of control.

To expand your horizons means that this tolerance encompasses the ability to listen openly to someone whose views are diametrically opposed to yours and then decide on your course of action. It is important not to compromise your basic principles.

Stretch your mind and find out what you enjoy in life and what you would profit from as a person.

DATE   IDEAS THAT I CAN USE

_____   _____

                   _____

                   _____

                   _____

                   _____

                   _____

                   _____

                   _____

                   _____

                   _____

SUMMARY:

1. "Bee" businesslike about your life.

2. Know what your life business is.

3. Know what you want to do with your life.

4. Design a life plan for yourself.

5. Be clear about your place in life.

6. Don't let life just happen.

7. Don't be afraid to try and try again.

8. Don't let the word *failure* enter your vocabulary.

9. Use outcomes to describe unsuccessful attempts.

10. Be specific about what you want.

10

ACT
ON YOUR DREAMS

What makes you feel fulfilled? What makes you happy? If you know what it is, you're lucky. If you don't, isn't it time you find out?

What makes dreams come true for some people and not so for others? Action. Talking about them is fine, visualizing is better, and day dreaming about them is fun, but none of these will make them come true. Only actions will!

If you want financial peace, success, and happiness in your life tomorrow, then act on your dreams today, Dream. Learn. Believe. Plan. Work. In these five steps devise a vision, a want. To learn is to gather knowledge about the thing wanted. To believe is to have faith that it is possible for you to have it. To plan is to draft a course of action for realizing your dream. To work is to labor the actions necessary to produce your dream.

To labor, to toil, to work, to produce results is the hardest part. It takes discipline to follow through on plans. Most of us are really not willing to work that hard! Most of us would like something for nothing. Generally, we all have a tendency to put off to tomorrow what we should do today and procrastinate reading a book on how not to procrastinate.

Discipline grinds on our nerves because we know it means work. Some of us are good starters but lose interest shortly thereafter. Some of us are good work horses; we can pick up in the middle but lose energy near the finishing line. Few of us are able to complete a project from start to finish.

It takes an Olympic type of thinking to excel. Most of us were not trained to be athletic about our lives. For most of us, life just happened! It was not a conscious plan laid out by our parents for us to follow. Most of the time we had no idea where we were going; we went along for the ride, going everywhere and nowhere.

It's been in recent years that people have become aware that life directions should be planned deliberately, that each moment of our lives can add up to something, something wonderful or something ordinary.

To make your life turn out wonderful takes mental self training equivalent to an athlete training. Your life should be as important as winning a game is for an athlete. After all, you want to win at life. You want to be the "star" of your life! Make discipline your ally, your partner in regulating your behavior. It will keep you in check. When you waiver, make excuses, or get lazy, discipline will put you back on course.

Discipline is a regular tool with successful people. The moments of their lives add up to success. Do yours? Realized moments are successions of fulfilled accomplishments. They make a more pleasant you. Unrealized moments are broken promises to yourself. They make you feel discouraged and depressed. You become dampened and sour on life.

Each day of your life should add up to something: peace, harmony, love, beauty, success, friendship, personal accomplishments, and universal harmony. It benefits you and those close to you to originate pleasant happenings. If you want happiness, then do something that will make you feel happy. If you want love, then be more loveable and friendly. If you want money, then produce results in your endeavors.

Harry, who was ready to divorce his wife, told his friend Fred, "I'll give her a dose of what she's been giving me!" Fred however suggested that Harry shower her with flowers and affection, then leave her! "That will get her!" Harry was surprised at the results when he employed his "Mr. Nice Guy" tactics. She was nice back! He couldn't live without her.

The Japanese have become economic giants due to similar practice of "Kyozan Kyoii - all mutually benefit and prosper." They start out their day showing appreciation for group effort. They know no man is an island. No rich man acquired his wealth alone. We all gain value from life whenever we add another to our life. No great battles were won alone!

Our American pioneering spirit, though necessary and admirable in early America, breeds isolation, struggle,and narrow gains. It is with the help of another that great feats are accomplished. Ask someone to help you reach your end. Don't be a martyr and struggle silently. Take chances and talk about your dreams. You'll be surprised how many people will show up to help you make it real.

Getting lost in dreams is good therapy. Thinking about tomorrow's dream takes the stress out of today's problem. Stress is a human instinct to fight or to flight. The human organism's heart beats faster, hormones change, adrenalin pumps up, blood switches from the skin areas to the larger vessels in the muscle regions and the body goes on alert, ready to do battle or escape to safety.

Know how much stress you can manage so when the course of the waters do not run smoothly, you'll know how much energy you have to expend, and still keep your equilibrium intact. In primitive times, man used the stress instincts to confront dinosaurs. Our present day dinosaurs are: financial pressure, work loads, relationship troubles, self-realization restraints, future responsibilities, etc. Talking with another about your dinosaurs helps. Maybe together you can find a way to tame and harness the dinosaur so that your reactions become diluted.

Train yourself to put less importance on them. One way to reduce stress is to look ahead to your future, to think on the way you want it to be. Today's climb will be made easier if you set your sights on tomorrow.

Another way to diffuse stress is to become physical: walk, run. etc. It gets rid of the pressure that is built up by your method of reacting to stress. You cause your own stress by the way you react to these dinosaurs.

The tolerance level for the amount of steam each can handle varies with each individual. When the level exceeds your saturation level, then you need to release it physically. Concentrate on staying loose like an athlete when the pressure crowds in on you. Athletes and dancers spend hours practicing to remove tension from their muscles so their bodies can produce their best act.

Stressful situations are opportunities to experience another dimension of living. Fill your mind with positive dreams during these times of trial. Tension of mind and body is the number one enemy in execution of any skill or act. Think about beautiful things when tension or worry shows up.

You can't help the way you feel, but you can help the way you think or act. We can change our lives by changing the attitudes of our minds. Life is merely an extension of our thoughts. Stress is a human instinct, a reaction to something that can be controlled.

Any thought or feeling held in the mind for a period of time becomes an attitude in one's thought processes. Your attitudes are reinforced by what you choose to see and believe. If you believe that you can't make your dreams come true, then you can't. Change your belief system by acting as if you can and in time you'll feel like you can. Let go of your doubts; they only hold you back.

What you hold in your mind will shape your experiences tomorrow. Let go of what you are today and agree to be that person you imagine yourself to be. Let go of what you are to become the person you want to be. Act out your new self-image until it feels real.

Dreams are making your longings real. It's the stuff that captures you fully: mentally, physically, emotionally. It's finding your own uniqueness and setting sail despite the obstacles that may befall you. It takes courage to be one's genuine self.

It is incredible how accurately your life reflects what you think about yourself. If you don't trust yourself, you'll have distrusting people around you. If you consider yourself unloveable, your associations will be insecure. You'll be demanding proof from them. If you want to get along with others, get along with yourself.

The ultimate source of success is to view your dilemmas as opportunities. Start acting out your dreams today. An action a day produces wonders. Do an action each day until it becomes a permanent habit. To feel important, act important. Ask yourself constantly, "What is the right thing to do?" Then do it.

DATE   IDEAS THAT I CAN USE

_____   _____

                  _____

                  _____

                  _____

                  _____

                  _____

                  _____

                  _____

                  _____

SUMMARY:
1. Know what makes you feel fulfilled.
2. Act on your dreams today.
3. Devise a vision of what you want.
4. Gather knowledge about your vision.
5. Believe that you can have it.
6. Plan a course of action.
7. Work to make it happen.
8. Make discipline a regular habit.
9. Take stress out of today's problems by thinking about tomorrow's dreams.
10. Become the person you'd like to be.

HELPFUL HINTS

Now that you have a tally on your finances, what do you do? How do you invest?

Practically speaking, live within your income. Pay yourself first. Save at least 10% of your pay every month. Build a reserve account for emergencies, and a needed relief fund if needed. Try not to spend this. Save at least three months pay before you start to invest. You can keep this money in CD's (Certificate of deposits — see your local bank for details) on a short term basis, and put them on a rotating basis, i.e. 1/3 in a savings account, 1/3 in C.D.'s, and 1/3 in C.D.'s with a different expiration date.

Pay down your credit cards. Make the normal monthly payment plus more — possibly $10, $20 or $30 extra. If you have to put something on a credit card, subtract this amount from your checking account, so when the bill arrives, you can pay off the purchase plus your monthly charge, plus an additional payment of $10, $20 or whatever you can afford at the time.

Pay off the credit cards that have the highest interest and look into credit cards with lower interest rates. Work slowly and methodically.

Do your homework before making any investment decisions. If you take a calculated risk, your chance for success can be heighten.

Good luck!

READING LIST

Bloodworth, Venice. *Key To Yourself.* Marina del Regy, CA: De Vorss & Company, 1952.

Carnegie, Dale. *How To Stop Worrying and Start Living.* New York: Simon and Schuster, 1984.

Christensen, James P. Combs, Clint Durrant, George D. *Rich On Any Income.* Salt Lake City, Utah: Shadow Mountain, 1985.

Hill, Napoleon. *Think and Grow Rich.* New York: Fawcett Press, 1963.

Lerner, Eugene M., Koff, Richard M. *Increasing Your Wealth.* Chicago, IL: Probus Publishing Co., 1985.

Cohen, Stanley J. & Wool, Robert. *How To Survive on $50,000 to $150,000 a Year.* New York: Penguin Books, 1984.

Graham, Benjamin. *The Intelligent Investor.* New York: Harper & Row, 1973.

Hay, Louise L. *You Can Heal Your Life.* Santa Monica, CA: Hay House, 1984.

Robbins, Anthony. *Unlimited Power.* New York: Fawcett Columbine, 1986.

Hubbard, Ron L. *Dianetics.* Los Angeles CA: Bridge Publications, Inc., 1985.

Train, John. *The Money Masters.* New York: Penguin Books Ltd., 1980.

Sinetar, Marsha. *Do What You Love, The Money Will Follow.* New York/Mahwah: Paulist Press, 1987.

Do you find it hard to get motivated about keeping a budget? Is it difficult even to think about organizing your bills and keeping current with everyday matters?

This humorous, yet helpful book will make the matter of money a fun activity. You will actually look forward to keeping abreast of your financial situation. Enjoy your new found success.

ORDER FORM

Please send me the necessary forms so that I can complete my financial profile. These worksheets will be mailed to:

Name _____

Address _____

City, State, Zip_____

In return, I will send a check or money order for $3.95 (Colorado residents add appropriate sales tax) to:

Far Isles Unlimited, Inc.
1630 30th St., Suite 253
Boulder, CO 80301